JK ROWLING

The Wizard Behind Harry Potter

JK ROWLING
The Wizard Behind Harry Potter

Marc Shapiro

JOHN BLAKE

Published by John Blake Publishing Ltd,
3 Bramber Court, 2 Bramber Road, London W14 9PB, England

ISBN 1 903402 33 6

British Library Cataloguing-in-Publication Data:
A catalogue record for this book is available from
the British Library.

Typeset by Jon Davies

Printed in England by CPD, Wales

1 3 5 7 9 10 8 6 4 2

Papers used by John Blake Publishing Ltd are natural, recyclable products
made from wood grown in sustainable forests. The manufacturing processes
conform to the environmental regulations of the country of origin.

Dedication

To all the good people.
My wife, Nancy. My daughter, Rachael.
My mother, Selma. My agent, Lori.
Bennie and Freda. Keri, Bad Baby, Chaos.
Mike Kirby, Steve Ross.

And finally to JK Rowling for lighting up
the imagination of a whole generation.
All good thoughts to you.

Acknowledgements

Since *Harry Potter* burst on the scene, JK Rowling has been the subject of many press articles and has given many interviews. I found the following publications, with their high level of professionalism, particularly helpful: *Current Biography*, the *Daily Telegraph*, *Time*, *Newsweek*, *Entertainment Weekly*, the *Boston Globe*, *Salon* magazine, the *New York Times*, the *Guardian*, the *Los Angeles Times*, *School Library Journal*, *Book* and *People*.

The following websites also helped in this journey: *JK Rowling: Raincoast Kids*; *Meet JK Rowling: Scholastic.com*; *JK Rowling: Bookwire*; *The Unofficial Harry Potter Fan Club Page*; *Harry Potter: Scholastic.com*; *The Essential Harry Potter*; books: *BBC*

Contents

INTRODUCTION

I LOVE TO READ

I confess, I love to read. After a hard day's work, there is no better way to wind down and relax than by curling up in a soft, comfortable chair, putting my feet up on an equally soft stool, and flipping through the pages of a good book as my cat, Chaos, purrs contentedly in my lap. What I read depends on what kind of mood I'm in.

Sometimes I want to find out about real people and real lives, so I will pick up a biography. But there are also those times when reading about the real world is the last thing on my mind. That is when I will pick up a science-fiction story, a spooky thriller, or a *Harry Potter* book — and escape to a place I've never been before.

There has always been a sense of comfort in escaping into a world of fantasy. Which is why the adventures of Harry Potter are so much fun for children and adults alike. There are, quite simply, no rules in a *Harry Potter* book — or at least none that cannot be broken in the name of fun and adventure.

We can have adventures in Harry's world that we cannot have anywhere else. As we flip through the pages of *Harry Potter and the Philosopher's Stone* or *Harry Potter and the Chamber of Secrets*, we can close our eyes and pretend we've just finished a rousing game of Quidditch and are now back in the hallowed halls of Hogwarts, learning the fine arts of charms, spells and magic, alongside good friends Ron and Hermione, at the feet of Professor Dumbledore.

Entering the world of Harry Potter is like following Alice down the rabbit hole into Wonderland. It is a place where just about anything can happen and usually does. Some of what goes on is truly frightening. I would not want to meet Voldemort or a Dementor on a dark night. But I sure would love to rip open a Howler and have it scream out its message to me. Travelling by way of Floo Powder would definintely beat being stuck in rush-hour traffic. And I doubt anyone could find a better friend than Ron or Hermione.

The sign of a good fantasy is when the reader can lose himself or herself in it. And it goes with out saying that millions of children and adults around the world have done just that through the adventures of Harry Potter.

But being curious, we also have questions. How did the author come up with those ideas? What does the person who created Harry look like? What colour is her hair? After we have enjoyed our trip to fantasyland, we eventually want to know all about her.

What is the person who writes the *Harry Potter* stories like? Is she young or old? Happy or sad? Does she live alone, or does she write these fantastic stories with a brood of children underfoot? Did she have a happy childhood or was her family life so unhappy she was driven to escape into the world of fantasy?

Those were the questions I wanted to have answered. Which is why I set out to write *JK Rowling: The Wizard Behind Harry Potter*.

Often, the story behind the author is as interesting, if not more so, than what is written. In the case of JK Rowling, the story has a little bit of everything. There is happiness and love. There is also some sadness. The story of JK Rowling is also one of bravery, determination, and triumph over seemingly overwhelming odds.

And, finally, there is the happy ending. The life of JK Rowling sounds very much like the stories she writes and is, in a way, a fairytale come to life. Knowing about JK Rowling and how she came to write the most popular books in the whole wide world will not change your feelings about Harry Potter. But a closer look at the wizardry of Harry Potter's creator will definitely give you the story behind the story.

And knowing more will only add to the enjoyment the next time you sit in your chair or crawl into bed and pull the covers up tight and disappear into the land of Harry Potter one more time.

I am back to my comfortable chair

and my good book.
    Chaos is purring.
    It is time to turn the page.

Marc Shapiro

1

WILD ABOUT HARRY

Sometimes the real world can be a confusing place. It is not always fair or kind. And in the real world there are not always happy endings. Which is why, every once in a while, we like to escape into the world of fantasy — a place where things always go our way and there is always a happy ending.

We want to believe in fantastic creatures in imaginary lands. We want to believe in magic powers, good friends and the power of good to triumph over evil. We all fantasize about being able to fly and lift buildings off the ground. And how good a magic sword would feel in our hand as we go off to slay a dragon or win the hand of a beautiful princess.

That is why we like Superman, Peter Pan, Mary Poppins and the amazing adventures of Frodo in *The Lord of the Rings*. And it is why we are all now Potterites who can't wait for the further adventures of our favourite wizard, Harry Potter, a 13-year-old English orphan who attends the Hogwarts School of Witchcraft and Wizardry and tries to be a normal boy while confronting the truly fantastic at every turn.

The author of the Harry Potter

books, JK (Joanne Kathleen) Rowling, is a grown woman with a child of her own. She is sensible, modest, and realistic — all good qualities when it comes to being a good parent and a positive member of the real world. She likes to walk the streets of her home town of Edinburgh, Scotland. She will sit for hours in her favourite café, sipping an espresso and watching as the world passes her by.

But there is something that sets JK Rowling apart from the rest of us. For Joanne Kathleen Rowling likes to dream at all hours of the day and night. She dreams of faraway lands, larger-than-life good guys, truly evil bad guys, and likeable young children who try and make sense of it all. But unlike others, she turns her dreams into reality when she sits down with pen and paper and begins to write about the adventures of Harry Potter.

A smile crosses her face. Her already expressive eyes, framed by long wavy hair, grow even wider. Her pen slashes across the paper like a lightning bolt. In her mind, a door to a delightful new world of imagination and wonder has just opened wide and she is about to pass through it.

When JK Rowling sits down to give new life to Harry Potter, usually in her favourite writing place, a café called Nicholson's, a change comes over the author. Because to create the latest adventure of Harry, his good friends Ron Weasley and Hermione Granger, and their adventures, Joanne has to stop being an adult and become a child who also wants to believe in the unbelievable.

And once Joanne becomes that child, almost anything can and does happen.

From the opening passages of *Harry Potter and the Philosopher's Stone*, we can sense that something quite out of the ordinary is up. Our introduction to Harry is not a happy one. He is an orphan who has been living for ten years in a closet under the stairs of his cruel aunt and uncle's house. But we soon discover that Harry is not an ordinary soul. He is the son of wizards. However, Harry does not have a clue that he even has these powers until one day a giant appears out of nowhere and delivers to Harry a scholarship to the Hogwarts School of Witchcraft and Wizardry.

Once there, Harry discovers friends, foes, his magical powers and a mission to get rid of the evil that lies hidden in the depths of the school. In the classic sense, friends unite, evil is banished — at least temporarily — and all is well.

There is much more of the same in *Harry Potter and the Chamber of Secrets*, as a more mature Harry and his friends once again battle evil while the young wizard begins to learn more about his adopted land. And what he finds, thanks to Joanne's vivid imagination, are surprises around every corner. There is the diary that writes back, a dead professor who continues to teach class, and portraits of long-dead ancestors who come alive at night to primp and curl their hair.

By the third book, *Harry Potter and the Prisoner of Azkaban*, the author has seen fit to darken the tone. In the Dementors, we see truly disgusting evil. But Harry has by this time grown wise enough and powerful enough to fight the good fight. There is also that priceless moment when Harry discovers Cho Chan on the Quidditch field and thinks to himself that she is quite pretty.

Joanne has filled the pages of Harry's adventures with enticing images and has us hooked.

'I really can, with no difficulty at all, think myself back to 11 years old,' said Rowling in a *Time* magazine interview of her ability to tap into her own childhood when writing. 'I can remember being a kid and being very powerless and having this whole underworld that to adults is always going to be impenetrable. I think that I have very vivid memories of how it felt to be Harry's age.'

On more than one occasion, Joanne has acknowledged her childhood memories as an influence. For her, Hermione is very much herself as a child. And while there was no real-life Harry in her life, she has said that many elements of the character have come from people she knew. And her enemies? They spring to life when Joanne remembers the times when she had to face the school bully and did not know whether she would emerge unscathed.

The author has said that what she likes about writing the adventures of Harry Potter, and what brings her willingly to the task every day, is the notion of opening up a world of dreams and its possibilities.

'When you dream, you can do what you like,' she has told *Newsweek*.

And there have been dreams aplenty in the first three Harry Potter adventures; *Harry Potter and the Philosopher's Stone* (retitled *Harry Potter and the Sorcerer's Stone* in America), *Harry Potter and the Chamber of Secrets*, and *Harry Potter and the Prisoner of Azkaban*. The world Harry Potter inhabits is dotted with strange creatures like Buckbeak, Scabbers and Crookshanks. There are good people like Professor Dumbledore and Hagrid and bad people like the Dursleys and the evil Lord Voldemort. In the world of Harry Potter, goblins run banks, apprentice students chase after balls on flying broomsticks, and wizards tread lightly as they enter the Forbidden Forest.

But finally it is Harry Potter, a skinny 13-year-old with glasses, green eyes and a head of unruly black hair who is the heart and soul of JK Rowling's adventures. The author feels that Harry is a mirror into her young readers' souls.

'Harry is smart and good at sports and a lot of things that other children would like to be,' Rowling once told an interviewer. 'But children also feel for him because he has lost his parents. If an author makes a character an orphan, few children will want to be an orphan, too. But it is a freeing thing because a certain weight of parental expectation is lifted.'

Yet the adventures of Harry Potter are much more than merely escapism for the preteen set. Adults have also taken Harry to their hearts and marvel at the simplicity and positive values presented in the tales. Harry is often the centre of a family's time together. Parents read to their children and children often read out loud to their parents. Or parents, after their children have gone to sleep, have been known to sit down with the book and read it themselves.

The author regularly reads her fan mail and is therefore well aware that the power of Harry Potter to capture readers has spanned the generations. A woman from Glasgow, Scotland, recently wrote to Joanne's British publisher asking how to go about joining the Harry Potter Fan Club, adding as an aside that she was 60 years old. An Englishman, when inquiring about the possibility of a Harry Potter movie, described himself as 'a child at heart, an adult in body'. She has had reports of family squabbles breaking out at bedtime when a parent wanted to finish reading a chapter and ended up taking the book from her children so she could read the book herself.

Joanne has thought long and hard about why people of all ages respond to Harry, and she thinks she knows the reason why.

'I think some of the reason is that Harry has to accept adult burdens in his life, although he is a child,' she said in a recent interview. 'There's something very endearing about that to kids and adults as well. Harry is also an old-fashioned hero. There's enough human frailty in Harry that people of all ages can identify with.'

The author also points to a sense of morality that runs through each book. Rather than preach, she gets her messages across quite naturally in the actions and thoughts of her characters. As we have discovered in the first four books, Harry Potter is not the perfect little boy. He bends and breaks the rules when it suits his purpose and has all the insecurities of a normal boy or girl. Children and adults tend to love the fact that they can open a *Harry Potter* book and see themselves in the characters.

Arthur Levine, the US editor of the *Harry Potter* books, feels that a big attraction to readers is the idea of growing up under-appreciated, feeling like an outcast, and then suddenly bursting forth into the light and being discovered. 'That is the fantasy of every person who grows up smart but not very athletic. That's the emotional connection that drew me to the books,' he told the *New York Times*.

Whatever the reason, *Harry Potter* has become a worldwide phenomenon since the publication of the first book in 1997. To date, the first four books have sold more than 10 million copies in over 100 different languages. The books continue to reside at or near the top of a number of bestseller lists, and a movie studio recently announced that it will be making a big-budget movie of *Harry Potter and the Philosopher's Stone* in the not-too-distant future.

But there is more to the popularity of *Harry Potter* than book sales and movie deals. Kids have taken Harry to their hearts, and he has become a very real part of their playtime. They have made up games and put on plays centring around Harry and his adventures. Many of the numerous websites that have sprung up around the *Harry Potter* books feature original stories written by fans. Groups of children gather regularly to read *Harry Potter* out loud. One enterprising 11-year-old even had 'Educated at Hogwarts' printed up on business cards so he could hand them out to his friends.

Surprisingly, the author behind the fantastic adventures of Harry Potter is a person of relatively simple pleasures and tastes. She told an Internet site that she has no hobbies 'except hanging out with my friends and writing'. Her favourite holiday is Hallowe'en. Her favourite television shows are British comedies and the US imports *Frasier* and *The Simpsons*.

'I get bored with my life,' she once said. 'I prefer inventing things.'

But for Rowling, the true joy comes in the stories of how young children have embraced her tales. And they certainly have. A family in California was so anxious to read *Harry Potter and the Prisoner of Azkaban* that they ordered a British copy of the book on the Internet so that they would not have to wait months for the book to be published in America. When her third book went on sale at 3.45pm, a time when most English schools finish lessons for the day, she was amazed when stores sold out of every copy in a matter of minutes.

Rowling, who is often shy about doing interviews and has proven very secretive when asked about the further adventures of Harry, came to enjoy book tours. In fact, she derives a lot of pleasure from book signings, when she gets to meet her young audience face-to-face. One example of this occurred during a visit to a school in England, when she was approached by a young boy carrying one of her books.

'He recited the first page of the first book to me from memory,' Rowling explained to *Newsweek*. 'When he stopped, he said, "I can go on." He continued reciting the first five pages of the book. That was unbelievable.'

However, she commented, one of her most gratifying moments came about during a reading and book signing appearance in Edinburgh.

'The event was sold out and the queue for signing at the end was very long. When a 12-year-old girl finally reached me, she said, "I didn't want there to be so many people here, because this is my book!" I told her that was exactly how I feel about my favourite books. Nobody else has a right to know them, let alone like them!'

What can best be described as Pottermania occurred last year when Joanne went to the USA on yet another book tour. Her many stops at bookstores across the country continued to amaze her and showed the author that while *Harry*

Potter books are written in a distinctly British style, the messages in her books are international.

During a reading in a high school gymnasium in Santa Rosa, California, Joanne was shocked when she looked out and saw 2,500 *Harry Potter* fans jumping up and down in their seats and shouting, 'Harry! Harry!' at the top of their lungs.

The scene repeated itself in San Francisco, California, when Joanne's car rounded a corner and the writer was amazed to find more than 1,000 people standing in line in front of a bookstore for a 9.30am reading and autograph session. She would later discover that many of the children and their parents had spent the night queuing just so they could make sure they would get in for the event. One family had even made the six-hour trip by car from Los Angeles the night before just so they could be first in line. Joanne gave a short reading, answered her fans' many questions, and then signed 1,000 books in two hours. And then, quick as a flash, she was back inside her limo and gone.

'It was a little like having the Beatles here,' said an excited, out-of-breath bookstore representative to *Entertainment Weekly* after the event. 'Kids will probably be coming here for years saying, "Wow! That's where the *Harry Potter* lady was standing."'

For JK Rowling, the success of *Harry Potter* has been a fantasy all of its own. After years of struggling in unfulfilling jobs, living in poverty, and trying to make a go of it as a single mother, the author now lives comfortably in Scotland and regularly travels around the world. She has often reflected on how her reaction to the success of Harry 'has been shock' and that 'it was like being catapulted into fairyland'.

'I always find it difficult to be objective about Harry,' she once admitted to *BBC Online* when discussing the question of reality and fantasy in her books. 'To me, they remain my own private little world. For five years, they were my own private secret. From the moment I had the idea for the book, I could see a lot of comic potential in the idea that wizards walk among us.'

But, finally, JK Rowling's success is a dream come true. 'I would have been crazy to have expected what has happened to Harry,' she has said. 'The mere fact of being able to say I was a published author was the fulfilment of a dream I've had since I was a very young child.'

2

RABBIT AND MISS BEE

JK Rowling's parents met on a train in 1963. And, as in all good fairytales, it was love at first sight.

A quick glance at them, and Peter Rowling and his bride-to-be could not have been more different. Peter was the manager of an aircraft factory, while Ann worked as a lab technician. He came from a blue-collar world, while she was into books and more intellectual pursuits. However, none of those differences seemed to matter.

Because, as they courted, fell in love and eventually decided to get married, they discovered that they did indeed have a lot in common. They shared a good sense of humour, and both believed in the importance of home and family life. They also loved the English countryside and good books.

When they walked down the aisle, Peter and Ann felt that they had each found the perfect mate.

Shortly after their marriage, Peter and Ann moved into a small but comfortable home in the tiny hamlet of Chipping Sodbury. The couple loved the idea of living literally in the middle of England's famed forests and hillsides. But they had always been city dwellers, so they enjoyed their regular trips into the nearby town of Bristol, where they would shop and idle away the hours together. The young couple felt they had the perfect life. Only one thing could enrich their story.

And that came about in November 1965, when the couple announced to family and friends that Ann was pregnant with their first child. The next nine months were a joyous and exciting time for Peter and Ann as they prepared for the arrival of their child. They speculated about whether their child would be a boy or a girl and discussed names for the child at great length. They regularly wandered into the room that had been picked out as the nursery and planned where the crib would be and what colours the walls should be painted. And as is true of all parents, they hoped that the child would be healthy and happy.

Late in July 1966, Peter's car pulled up in front of Chipping Sodbury General Hospital. It was time.

Joanne Kathleen Rowling came

kicking and screaming into the world on 31 July 1966. In later years, Joanne would look back on the occasion of her birth as an omen of things to come. 'I think it is rather appropriate for someone who collects funny names to be born in a hospital named Chipping Sodbury,' she laughed.

Almost from the moment Joanne was born, Peter and Ann sensed the bright, inquisitive nature of their daughter. Her eyes were always wide in amazement at the world around her, and she was always grasping and touching things with curiosity. They could almost predict that one of the first words out of their daughter's mouth would be 'Why?'

Joanne once described her early childhood years as 'dreamy'. The young child seemed to have a knack for solitary pursuits. She often played imaginary games in her room or in the tall grass in her garden. If there was a tree around, she would climb it. If other children approached her, Joanne was quick to invite them to join her in any number of games. Even in those early years, she was very fond of the idea of 'let's pretend'.

Hoping to nurture Joanne's imagination, her parents began reading to her at an early age. Because both parents were constant readers, it is no surprise that one of the author's earliest memories was of 'the house being full of books and of my parents constantly reading to me'. Joanne was fed a steady diet of fairytales and fantasy stories as well as a smattering of the classics. Even during her most uncomfortable moments, the sounds of her parents reading to her always had a calming effect.

'My most vivid memory of childhood is my father sitting and reading *The Wind in the Willows* to me,' she told the *Daily Telegraph*. 'I had the measles at the time, but I don't really remember that. I just remember the book.'

What her parents did not realise was

that a constant exposure to literature — in particular, to fairytales and stories of the fantastic — had made an enormous impression on the young child. She began to dream up fantastic, well-plotted stories with larger-than-life characters. When she was at play, her stories were full of character and detail, light-years beyond those generally produced by a child of her age.

Although she was too young to think in terms of what she wanted to be when she grew up, Joanne Kathleen Rowling, at a very early age, had this image of herself as somebody who would put pencil to paper and create magic worlds. 'Writing for me has always been a kind of wonderful compulsion,' she said in a 1999 interview. 'I don't think anyone could have made me do it or could have prevented me from doing it. It's weird, but writing is all I ever wanted to do.'

But these were private thoughts for Joanne, that wonderful secret that kept her warm and cosy in her bed at night and helped her to glide through her days. To tell even her parents would have ended all the fun.

But when her younger sister, Di, born less than two years after Joanne, reached three years old, five-year-old Joanne began making up tall tales about fantastic creatures and imaginary places and telling them to Di.

These stories would often centre on rabbits because, as Joanne has recalled, 'we badly wanted a rabbit'. One of the most memorable of these early flights of fantasy, and the one that always had Di roaring with little-girl laughter and excitement, was a story about how Di had fallen down a rabbit hole one day and ended up being fed strawberries by the rabbit family.

More often than not, Di would sit enthralled by her older sister's tales. She would inevitably ask Joanne to tell her the same story again and again, and because the stories were not written down, they would often come out slightly different in the retelling. Joanne was encouraged by her younger sister's response to begin jotting her stories down on paper. So, one day, not long after she turned six, Joanne sat down with pencil and paper and wrote her first story.

Not surprisingly, it was a story about a rabbit called Rabbit, who caught the measles and was visited by a number of friends, including a giant bee named Miss Bee.

'I wrote stories about rabbits for a couple of years. I definitely had a rabbit fixation,' Joanne once told an interviewer.

Di was thrilled with the story. Joanne's parents, who had taken to eavesdropping on their daughter's fantasies, were amused by their daughter's imagination but did not feel it necessary to involve themselves actively in any way. Their encouragement would have been superfluous anyway, because Joanne had already made up her mind that she was going to be a writer.

'Ever since Rabbit and Miss Bee, I knew I wanted to be a writer,' she told *School Library Journal*. 'I cannot overstate how much I wanted that. But I would rarely tell anyone so. I just never really spoke about it because I was embarrassed, and because my parents were the kind of parents who would have thought, Ah yes, that's very nice, dear. But where is the pension plan?'

Joanne grew into a bright child whose imagination was often the talk of the neighbourhood. This talent was also a topic during her first years at school, when her teachers would marvel at the maturity and creativity of her early stories and essays. Joanne took these early compliments as a sign that she had found something she was good at.

Another one of the young girl's early attempts at storytelling was a story of chills and adventure called *The Seven Cursed Diamonds*.

'At that age, I thought it was a novel,' she would recall in later years. 'But I think now that it was only a very long short story.'

And Joanne enjoyed more than just writing her own stories during those early years; her parents usually found her nose buried in the stories of others. The young child was quite outgoing and had a number of friends in the neighbourhood, but always seemed to prefer going off by herself and reading. Among her favourites was *The Little White Horse* by Elizabeth Goudge, *Manxmouse* by Paul Gallico, and the Narnia books by CS Lewis.

'I adored E Nesbit,' Joanne once said of her reading habits. 'I think her books are wonderful. I also liked Noel Streatfield, who did those girly books about ballet shoes and things. Even now, if I was in a room with one of the Narnia books, I would pick it up and re-read it like a shot,' she explained to the *Daily Telegraph*.

Shortly after Joanne began to write, her parents decided that they needed a bigger home and moved the family to the small town of Yate, just outside Bristol. Less than a year after that move, Peter and Ann decided that they liked the scenery better on the other side of Bristol and moved the family to yet another small town — Winterbourne. .

Joanne and Di quickly adjusted to the moves and made friends easily with the local children. Winterbourne, in particular, was home to a lot of children Joanne and Di's age; they were immediately welcomed into the informal gang that would play games up and down the streets of the town. In those days, Joanne was very much a tomboy, engaging in just about every rough-and-tumble game without worrying about falling over and hurting herself. Even at that age, Joanne was not what you would call athletic and would often fall. But her willingness to have a go soon gained her the respect of her new friends.

Two of her closest friends in Winterbourne were a brother and sister named Ian and Vikki Potter. In later years, Ian Potter would tell *Book* magazine that when his sister and he would get together with Joanne and Di, they would occasionally tell stories.

'But most of all we liked dressing up and, nine times out of ten, it would be Joanne who would say, "Oh, let's play witches and wizards."'

Joanne remembered being quite close to Ian and Vikki during their days in Winterbourne. One reason for their friendship was their name.

'Their surname was Potter,' she once recalled. 'I always liked the name.'

3

CHILDISH THINGS

Shortly after Joanne Kathleen Rowling's ninth birthday, her parents decided it was time to move once again. Only this time it was because her parents' dream had finally come true.

Peter and Ann Rowling had both been born and raised in London and were basically city folk at heart. But because it was cheaper to live in the country, they had postponed any notion of living in a city. However, as Peter gained promotion at his car factory and began receiving a higher salary, the couple decided it was time to make the move.

The couple, despite their yearning for city life, had grown to enjoy the proximity of the countryside. Rather than a big city, the Rowlings decided smaller would be better.

Tutshill is a small town situated near Chepstow in the Forest of Dean. It was very much a bustling town with streets, stores and schools. But the river Wye ran through it and there were fields all around, making it the ideal mixture of city and country.

Joanne and Di quickly adjusted to their new surroundings. They would frolic for hours by the river and make up fantasy games to act out in the fields. Joanne was outgoing and soon made friends in her neighbourhood. When she felt comfortable enough, she would bring out some of her stories and read them to the local kids. While the other children did not quite know what to make of this little girl who used big words and told funny stories about fantastic places, they were impressed and gladly made room for a regular storytime from Joanne.

She would continue to enjoy playground activities, but reading and writing, which are solitary pursuits, remained first on her list of passions.

When it came to books, she was already reading well beyond her class at school. At nine years old, Joanne discovered Ian Fleming's James Bond novels, and they became a regular part of her reading list.

Not too long after that, she discovered the works of Jane Austen and was never the same again. Austen's delicate passages and detailed stories became a model for Joanne Rowling. 'Jane Austen is my favourite author ... ever.'

There was only one drawback to

living in the town of Tutshill — Joanne had to go to Tutshill Primary School, and she hated it.

'It was a very small, very old-fashioned place,' she painfully remembered for the *Okubooks* website. 'The rolltop desks still had inkwells.'

But that was not the only problem Joanne had with the school. There was a new teacher to deal with. And this teacher scared the life out of Joanne. She was a strict, no-nonsense type who taught her class according to the book. Unfortunately for Joanne, the teacher's book and her new student did not agree when it came to certain subjects.

'She gave me a test on the very first morning and, after a huge effort, I managed to get zero out of ten,' she said.

On her first day, the teacher sat Joanne in a row of desks to the far right of the classroom. The young child was fine with that until a few days later when she figured out, by talking to her fellow students, that the teacher had put her in the 'stupid' row.

It seemed that the teacher had made up her seating chart based on how clever she thought her students were. The brightest students sat on the left side of the room and the rest sat on the right. Joanne painfully recalled her first days at Tutshill Primary when, she wrote, 'I was as far right as I could get without sitting on the playground.'

It was a tough first year for Joanne. She was not making friends as easily as she had in the past. Physically and emotionally she was changing. It all added up to a rough beginning at her new school.

'I wasn't as clever as I thought I should be,' she confessed when looking back on those days for *Salon* magazine. 'I don't think I was a know-all. I was obsessed with achieving academically, but that masked a huge insecurity. I think it is very common for plain young girls to feel this way. I definitely would not want to go back and do childhood again. I don't look back on it as a phase of blissful happiness at all.'

She was the new kid in school, and she had to deal with the embarrassment of being identified as 'dumb'. But Joanne managed to turn the experience around.

She studied hard and managed to make a small but loyal circle of friends. Not surprisingly, English was her best subject. Although she continued to write fantasy fables in her spare moments, she was not comfortable with sharing them with anyone but Di and one or two of her closest friends.

Joanne was determined to prove her teacher's impression of her wrong. By the end of the year, she had convinced the teacher that she was not by any means 'slow'. One day she was rewarded when her teacher told her she could now sit on the left side of the classroom. Joanne recalled the promotion with mixed emotions.

'I had been promoted to second left. But the promotion was at a cost. My teacher made me swap seats with my best friend. So in one short walk across the room, I became clever but unpopular,' Joanne recalled.

Joanne regained her popularity and continued through her primary school years in an uneventful way. Her grades continued to be good. She remained painfully shy, with only a small circle of close friends. And writing continued to be her passion.

No matter how busy her days were, she always managed to find some quiet time to release her fantasies. Her stories, full of magic and strange characters with funny names, were the highlight of her sister's playtime. The praise Joanne received from Di and her parents convinced Joanne, even as young as she was, that she would one day be an important writer and would live a wonderful, fairytale life.

Joanne successfully graduated from Tutshill Primary and was soon on her way to

Wyedean Comprehensive School. The confidence and positive self-image that Joanne had fought hard to cultivate throughout her junior school disappeared during her first year at Wyedean.

She became insecure at the prospect of attending school with older children, and she was going through puberty and thus felt very self-conscious. It also did not help that she wore glasses. 'I was quiet, freckly, short-sighted and rubbish at sports,' she commented.

But Joanne managed to find her niche at Wyedean. Eventually, she found other girls like her — quiet, smart and on the fringes of being popular — and she became a part of that group. She did quite well at school, with English and foreign languages being her favourite subjects.

The youngster slowly began to come out of her shell at Wyedean. She was continuing to write and finally felt confident enough to risk it all by reading some of her stories to her new friends. They liked what they heard and were regularly entertained by Joanne's creative efforts.

'I used to tell my equally quiet and studious friends long serial stories during lunchtime,' she wrote in an essay. 'They usually involved us all doing heroic and daring deeds we certainly would not have done in real life.'

Joanne breezed through her comprehensive school years on a steady course with relatively few noteworthy achievements. There was the embarrassment of breaking her arm one day while playing the non-contact sport of netball. There was also the day Joanne finally came of age at school when she was attacked by the toughest girl in her year. She would later recall that she would logically have preferred to run from trouble rather than stand and fight. But fight back is exactly what she ended up doing.

'I didn't have a choice,' she said. 'It

was hit back or lie down and play dead. For a few days, I was quite famous because she hadn't managed to flatten me. The truth was, my locker was right behind me and it held me up.'

Unfortunately, Joanne's new-found reputation as a tough girl lasted only a short time. She soon reverted to timidity and would spend weeks peering nervously around corners, in constant fear of being ambushed.

Through her later years at the comprehensive school, Joanne began to come out of her shell. Her confidence growing, she was now quicker to speak up in class and was more assertive in social conversations and activities. While still what would be considered very unathletic, she was now more inclined to assert herself with the other girls. This, she would later report, was due in part to the fact that her glasses had been replaced by contact lenses, so she was less fearful of being hit in the face.

In fact, Joanne, by her own reports, flowered in her teen years. She felt that, personally and socially, things had actually begun to get better and she finally came to the all-important realisation that there was more to Joanne Kathleen Rowling than someone who was driven to get everything right. Joanne was suddenly much more comfortable with herself.

Like most teenagers, Joanne had a growing sense of independence; this would lead to the occasional row with her parents, usually short-lived arguments over trivial matters. Her relationship with Di remained close. When not helping her younger sibling with her homework, Joanne would continue to use Di as her first audience for the many stories she was continuing to write. The second group to hear her latest tales was her girlfriends at school.

Despite the fact that she had numerous teachers who saw something in her and encouraged her in a creative direction, writing remained a largely private pursuit. The stories she felt confident enough to share were often the tales of action and adventure that featured herself and her friends as thinly-disguised characters in stories of derring-do.

Her other stories, those she perceived as more intimate, she would not show to anyone. These were the stories that she felt a real writer would write. And she was not quite ready to let the outside world into that part of her creative life.

Joanne's love for reading continued to blossom as well. She had long since begun to read about the lives of real people and had developed a particular infatuation for the author Jessica Mitford, a feminist who ran off and joined the Spanish Civil War at 19 and was a passionate supporter of human rights.

'I remember reading the book *Hons and Rebels* at 14, and it changed my life.'

Joanne had grown into quite the confident student in her senior year at Wyedean Comprehensive. She was popular and outgoing, and her grades were quite good. So good, in fact, that Joanne was appointed Head Girl in her final year.

Head Girl was a lofty position to which all the girls aspired. But, in fact, very little responsibility was attached to the role. Once a year, when some dignatory from the region came to visit the school, it was the job of the Head Girl to show her around the school fair. The requirement that Joanne dreaded the most was that the Head Girl also had to give a talk to the whole school.

'I decided to play them a record to cut down on the time that I had to speak to them,' she laughingly recalled. 'Well, the record was scratched, and right in the middle of playing, it began skipping and played the same line over and over again. Finally, the Deputy Headmistress came out on stage and kicked it.'

Joanne ended her years at Wyedean Comprehensive with high honours. Her teachers were predicting a bright future for her. Her parents were proud. Joanne Kathleen Rowling was quiet on the subject of her future. She knew in her heart of hearts what she wanted to do with her life. She had her own hopes and dreams.

Now all she had to do was figure out how to make them come true.

4

LIFE LESSONS

Joanne wanted to write. But being admittedly 'the most disorganised person in the whole world', she did not know how to begin. So she would write something, read through it, and usually find enough fault in her work to discard it. Even when she was happy with a story, it still remained her own private happiness.

She had boxes and folders full of

short stories, but did not have a clue how one went about getting them published. She knew magazines bought such stories all the time but never saw fit to submit one. Even thinking about doing so usually ended up with Joanne backing down in the face of her old fears of letting other people judge her work.

So, like so many others, Joanne was an 18-year-old with definite ideas but lacking the courage to carry them out. This was a side of herself that Joanne did not particularly like, and she would often upbraid herself for being too cowardly to challenge herself. But the truth was that Joanne Kathleen Rowling was just not ready to take on the world.

Because Joanne was frustrated at her inability to take that next big step in her writing life, she was easily influenced by others. Consequently, she was willing to take her parents' advice.

Peter and Ann, having not been

privy to her writing ambitions, had long been bewildered at their eldest daughter's seeming lack of direction. Joanne's parents had regularly suggested that with her love of language, their daughter should study French and literature, which would lead to a wonderful career as a bilingual legal secretary. And with her good grades, they felt Exeter University would be the ideal place for her to go.

Joanne's heart, though, was in her writing and she felt that pursuing any other line of work would be a mistake. However, being an obedient child, Joanne reluctantly took her parents' advice and was soon enrolled at Exeter.

The teenager was encouraged by the stories she had heard that Exeter was a liberal establishment that was big on unconventional ideas. She figured that, if nothing else, she would find much to influence her in her true passions. In fact, what she discovered shortly after enrolling was that Exeter was actually quite conservative, wrapped up in traditional ideals.

'It was fantastic,' she told a reporter, 'but it did not offer quite the chance to be a radical that I planned.'

Joanne's years at Exeter were productive. She found that she was able to master French fairly easily. A big part of her education at Exeter was a year spent in Paris, learning to use the French language in a practical setting. Joanne found the year abroad exhilarating.

She took in the sights and marvelled at being in another country for the first time without her family. Joanne grew up during that year in Paris. By the time she returned to Exeter, Joanne Kathleen Rowling had grown confident in her ability to make her way in the world.

During this time, Joanne had her first serious relationship. Being in love and having someone care about her was an important thing for her. Joanne revelled in the fact that she was, in fact, attractive enough and bright enough to gain the affections of a loving partner.

Of course, every spare moment was taken up with writing. There was the usual batch of short stories that only a handful of people ever saw. She also attempted a novel. But while she was confident in other areas, Joanne steadfastly refused to submit any of her stories, belittling them whenever anyone would suggest that her stories were good and that she should send them out.

This lack of confidence in the thing she valued most haunted her every waking hour. In her heart, Joanne knew that it was time to shake off the doubts. Unfortunately, her head still had a firm hold on her fears and insecurities. So she continued to do nothing at all.

Joanne graduated from Exeter with honours and, as often happens, she and her boyfriend naturally drifted apart. But Joanne had little time to grieve over a lost love. She was soon doing the rounds of her first job interviews.

Getting dressed up and presenting herself at job interviews was not something the young woman liked doing. It seemed like a silly, unnecessary game. It made her feel totally inadequate and very much like a little girl again. Besides, this was not what she really wanted to do, which was to write fabulous stories, see them published, be able to keep writing and live happily ever after. But since she was not willing to take the risks necessary to reach that pinnacle, Joanne had to contend with the real world.

The next six years were a rough introduction to the often tedious life of the workaday world. Joanne went through a series of jobs. In one instance, she spent two years researching human rights violations for Amnesty International. While she felt she was doing important work and that her idol, Jessica Mitford, would approve, the work itself soon became predictable and boring, two things Joanne could not abide.

For the most part, she undertook a seemingly endless string of boring secretarial jobs. The work did not interest her and she was not making a lot of money. Additionally, as she has readily admitted, 'I later proved to be the worst secretary ever.'

Her mind always seemed to be on something else. 'Whatever job I had, I was always writing like crazy,' she confided. 'All I ever liked about offices was being able to type up stories on the computer when no one was looking. I was never paying much attention in meetings because I was usually scribbling bits of my latest stories in the margins of the pad or thinking up names for my characters. This is a problem when you're supposed to be taking the minutes of the meeting.'

Needless to say, Joanne's employers frowned on her writing fantasy stories during company time, and she was dismissed from a couple of her jobs. But for the most part, Joanne simply got tired of doing work she detested and would eventually quit. Well into her twenties, the young woman was like a boat without a rudder.

Joanne's parents were supportive but concerned that their eldest daughter seemed to be having trouble finding her place in life. Her only solace in an otherwise bleak world was her writing.

'I was writing a lot of short stories and a lot of started and abandoned novels,' she told *School Library Journal*. 'I felt I worked very hard and had served my apprenticeship in terms of writing.'

She felt less than positive about herself when those works would inevitably end up in a box with all the other stories that had not seen the light of day.

Unfortunately, all the hard work still did not add up to much, so Joanne reluctantly searched for yet another job. This time she found employment as an office worker for the Manchester Chamber of Commerce.

Joanne had another reason for going to Manchester. She had received a letter from her old boyfriend at Exeter, stating that he was in Manchester and that he'd like to see her again. The job she got was as dull and boring to her as all the others had been, but this time she was determined to make a go of things.

Joanne made time for her old boyfriend but remained diligent in her writing. At lunchtime, she would make her way to one of the nearby pubs or cafés, settle at an out-of-the-way table, and write. While far from anti-social, she would often find herself praying that nobody in the office was having a birthday or some other celebration that would require her to join in, taking up her precious writing time.

Joanne looked upon the travelling between London and Manchester as her private time. She would often while away the time reading a book, working on her latest story, or simply staring out of the window at the passing scenery. One day, as she returned to London after yet another day of unrewarding work, the train suddenly ground to a halt.

There was some kind of mechanical problem that, it was announced, would require a delay of about four hours. Normally this would have been ideal. But since Joanne was too tired to either read or write, she focused her attention on a group of cows, grazing in a meadow in front of her.

What she did not realise was that her life was about to change.

'I was sitting on the train, just staring out the window at some cows — it was not the most inspiring subject — when all of a sudden the idea for Harry just appeared in my mind's eye. I can't tell you why or what triggered it. But I saw the idea of Harry and the wizard school very plainly.

I suddenly had this basic idea of a boy who didn't know what he was,' she remarked.

Joanne was enthralled with the vision that had come to her. She immediately reached for a pen and paper to begin jotting down notes and thoughts. Unfortunately, Joanne had neither. And so, with nothing but her memory to serve her, she sat quietly and just played with the notion of characters, funny names, and story possibilities.

By the time her train stopped at King's Cross station in London, Joanne had laid down the basic premise of the first *Harry Potter* story. Over the next few weeks and months, Joanne put every free moment into jotting down ideas and stories based on this imaginary boy and his adventures in a world ruled by magic. The *Harry Potter* files soon filled one box, then several.

Joanne continued her job at the Manchester Chamber of Commerce but took every opportunity before, during, and after work to fashion a single storyline for the first *Harry Potter* book. Soon, she came up with Harry, an orphan, being raised by a cruel aunt and uncle. He then finds out he is a wizard and is whisked off to a boarding school for young wizards called Hogwarts.

Joanne would often find herself smiling as she devised adventures for Harry and unusual names for the characters who would populate his world. Her whole outlook improved once she was inspired by Harry. Her parents and sister noticed the change, but they knew little about its cause. Joanne dropped little hints about something she was working on but stopped short of revealing the details. She felt that to let too much out would blunt the magic.

Joanne Kathleen Rowling was already thinking like a resident of Harry Potter's world.

But this period of good spirits would be short-lived. Her mother, who had been diagnosed with multiple sclerosis in the previous year, died suddenly at the age of 45.

Joanne was devastated. She was well aware that her mother had been ill but had no idea that MS would take her so quickly, and she felt terribly guilty that she had not been there in her mother's final hours. Her deepest regret was that she had never let her mother read any of Harry.

In her distracted state of mind, the young girl had a tough time concentrating on work, so soon afterwards, Joanne lost her job at the Manchester Chamber of Commerce.

'It was a nightmare period,' sighed Joanne. She told *People* magazine that writing about Harry was the only thing that got her through it.

5

HARRY IS BORN

*J*oanne was in an emotional turmoil. She had just turned 26. She was once again out of work, and the relationship with her boyfriend seemed to be going nowhere. And she felt consistently depressed and upset because of the death of her mother.

The only real joy in Joanne's life was Harry Potter. She had continued to work diligently on his adventures, with boxes overflowing with ideas, names and fragments of stories. Joanne was feeling confident about what she had jotted down and began seriously contemplating writing the novel. But she was torn between living out her dream of a life dedicated to writing and the guilt she was feeling at not being like everyone else.

Joanne was thinking very hard about what her life was about and what she wanted to do with it. One of the bright spots she kept coming back to was that year she had spent in Paris working as an assistant teacher. She had enjoyed it and thought she might enjoy it again. In any case, she felt she needed to do something constructive with her life.

Joanne's dreams of teaching in some far-off land finally won out. In September 1990, she announced to her family and friends that she would no longer settle for menial office work and soon accepted the offer of a job abroad, teaching English as a second language at a school in the northern Portuguese town of Oporto. Joanne was both excited and frightened at the prospect of going so far away to work, but she felt that being away from home and family was the only way she would ultimately find herself.

So she packed her bags, many of which contained her notes on Harry, kissed her father and sister goodbye and promised them she would write on a regular basis. Before she knew it, she was on her way.

Although she was homesick, Joanne quickly adjusted to life in Portugal. She immediately found a comfortable apartment and became well acquainted with the country, its people and its customs. She loved walking the quaint streets, window shopping and coming to terms with some of the more unusual Portuguese delicacies, such as tripe (the stomach lining of a cow). The people were friendly and it was sunny and warm all the time, a real contrast to the gloomy, cold weather in London. After a short while, the homesickness disappeared and Joanne settled into her teacher role.

Joanne's students took an immediate liking to her. And when they were not making fun of her name, calling her 'Rolling Stone', they would sit in rapt attention as Joanne taught them the fine art of speaking English. The transplanted Londoner was happy with the progress her students were making and proud of the good notices she had been receiving from the school superiors. She was also happy that her schedule allowed her to continue to write. 'I worked afternoons and evenings,' she recalled, 'and so I had my mornings free to write.'

Harry and his adventures at Hogwarts were slowly but surely coming together. The first pages of the novel were written on a wave of excitement. Joanne was discovering Harry much in the manner that her creation was discovering his magic — in short bursts of enthusiasm that often had her breaking into a spontaneous grin as the words flowed from her mind to the page.

She would chuckle as the names Hermione, Ron, Hagrid and Dumbledore instantly became immortalised in the shapes of Harry's many fantastic friends. Naming her characters was one of the most enjoyable parts about writing Harry. Having long been a collector of unusual names and clever when it came to creating her own, Joanne would often laugh uncontrollably when the likes of a Every Flavour Beans or a Justin Finch Fletchey would spring spotaneously to mind.

'Having a child who escapes the confines of the adult world and goes somewhere where he has power really appealed to me,' the author once revealed to the *Boston Globe* of her feelings while writing the first *Harry Potter* book. 'There's always room for a story that can transport readers to another place.'

But the excitement was often tempered by the frustration of trying to get everything about Harry and his world just right. The author admitted to some tears in those early days when, in detailing Harry's life as an orphan, she was forced to deal with the passing of her own mother.

Evil was also a notion that Joanne had to deal with when creating the villainous Lord Voldemort. Rather than create baddies typical of a children's book — noisy but not truly evil — she decided that evil in the world of *Harry Potter* would ring true to readers only if it was serious and its consequences befell the characters that the readers loved.

Ultimately, one aspect that caused Joanne the most concern was the tone of the books. From the beginning, Joanne was torn between writing the typical children's book, which often condescended to the

reader, or simply writing the book that she would choose to read as an adult. Joanne chose the latter course.

Writing this book, despite the obstacles and challenges involved, was a constant joy — one that would help her through her occasional bouts of loneliness. Joanne was friendly and outgoing with her co-workers but had remained reserved and shy around men. Despite having had a boyfriend at Exeter University, she had never thought of herself as pretty and so had never been too concerned that the years were rolling by without the prospects of a husband or a family in her life.

But all of that changed the day Joanne Kathleen Rowling fell in love.

She met him by chance. He was a journalist for one of the leading television stations in Portugal. Joanne, blushing like a schoolgirl, had been instantly attracted to his bright smile and his dark good looks. As they began to see each other, Joanne also discovered that he was bright, sensitive and interested in her.

Theirs was a whirlwind courtship. Within months of their meeting, Joanne and her handsome Portuguese lover were married.

The first two years of their marriage were good, if somewhat hectic, times for the couple. Her husband's work often kept him out until all hours and, with her schedule, they often found it difficult to find private time together. Still, Joanne found inspiration in her happiness, and it showed in her enthusiasm for her work and the continued progress of *Harry Potter*.

What had started out as a simple tale for young children was becoming more complex. What was intended as a book for young people was beginning to take on layers of depth equally suitable for adult readers. The characters were living and breathing in a very real way; although children, they were making difficult decisions and behaving much more maturely than most characters in children's stories. And so it did not bother Joanne when Harry's adventures in Hogwarts developed, with no end in sight.

In 1992, Joanne discovered that she was pregnant. The young couple were thrilled and, privately, the mother-to-be hoped that the prospect of a baby in the house would help their relationship, which had hit a rough patch.

Sadly, the pressures of married life, coupled with all the physical and emotional demands of the pregnancy, soon began to weigh on Joanne. In her mind, her husband was always at work and was not showing her the same consideration she had first experienced. Joanne would often lapse into fits of depression. There were tears. Her husband did his best to comfort her, but to no avail. Unfortunately, the birth of the couple's daughter, Jessica, in 1993, did little to save the crumbling marriage.

'I was very depressed,' Joanne remembered painfully in a *UK News* interview. 'And having a newborn child made it doubly difficult. I simply felt like a non-person. I was very low and I felt I had to achieve something.'

In a matter of weeks, Joanne and her husband divorced. She has been rather secretive about her marriage, refusing to reveal the name of her husband or the actual reason for the divorce. She would only concede that 'I've made my mistakes in that area. Just because you've got a good brain doesn't mean you're any better than the next person at keeping your hormones under control.'

Joanne found herself in a terrible state. She felt there was no reason to stay in Portugal, where the memory of her failed marriage would continue to haunt her and her prospects for any kind of life as a recently divorced woman with a child were limited. She was prepared to return to

London, although the idea of returning home as a divorced single mother was not something she was looking forward to doing.

Joanne remained quiet and withdrawn in those days following the divorce. She was there for her daughter in every possible way. But she cried at the drop of a hat. And the worst part of all was that she rarely worked on the book.

In the midst of this depression, she received a telephone call from her sister, who was now living in Edinburgh. Di suggested that Joanne might want to move to Edinburgh so that she could be near her family while she decided what she would do next. Joanne agreed, taking Jessica, her bags and the by now three chapters of *Harry Potter and the Philosopher's Stone*, and hopped on a train to Edinburgh. The journey was long and lonely. As the weather turned from bright sunshine to dark and foreboding, Joanne noted that it reflected her mood perfectly.

Although she was happy to be near her sister, once she arrived in Edinburgh, Joanne once again fell into deep despair. 'I had a tiny baby, no job, and I was in a strange place,' she painfully reflected in *People*.

These were not the best of times to be a single woman with a child in the UK. Just a month earlier, the British Prime Minister, John Major, had given a speech criticising single parents for being welfare-loving freeloaders. Joanne felt particularly offended by that speech. Yes, she was a single mother with a child. But she was also a college graduate with no shortage of skills. Certainly she would be able to keep her head above water.

But as she walked around Edinburgh with Jessica, Joanne often felt the hard stares of strangers. It was as if they knew.

A guardian angel named Sean appeared and loaned Joanne enough money to put a deposit down on what she once called 'a grotty flat'. With a roof over their heads, Joanne faced the dilemma of what to do. Her heart was set on finishing the *Harry Potter* book. But her dream was now complicated by the tiny bundle of joy asleep in her crib.

'I was terrified that I just wouldn't be able to justify to myself continuing to write,' she told *School Library Journal*. 'I thought it would benefit my daughter if I could earn a better living doing something else. If writing wasn't helping to buy new shoes, then it just felt very self-indulgent. What I was praying for was just to make enough for me to continue to write.'

Christmas was fast approaching and the festivities of the season only seemed to make Joanne feel worse. She had no money for presents for her daughter and the dear friends who had been there for her. Joanne felt coming to Edinburgh had been a hasty decision, so she made plans to return to

London and attempt to find another job after the new year.

One rainy afternoon, as she was visiting her sister, Joanne, on an impulse, began telling her sister the story of Harry Potter, much as she had the story of Rabbit years before. Di was immediately caught by the story and insisted that her older sister show her what she had written.

'It's possible that if she had not laughed, I would have set the whole thing to one side,' recalled Joanne in the *Daily Telegraph*.

'But Di did laugh.'

6

DARK AND LIGHT

Making her sister laugh was the first positive experience Joanne had had in a long time. Encouraged that she might be on the right track with her book, Joanne made what she hoped would be a smart choice.

Joanne knew she would have no trouble finding another teaching job. But to do that would mean there would be no time left for writing. Finally she decided that she would finish the book in a year and try to get it published.

Joanne knew that this was a step that, once taken, could not be reversed. She was deliberately setting herself up for a hard time. But she also realised that she had spent years sitting on the fence about her writing, to no avail. To take a chance now would not put her in any worse a predicament then she was already in.

'I thought, What is the worst that could happen? Every publishing company in Britain could turn me down. Big deal,' she explained to the *Daily Telegraph*.

Thinking that gave the young mother strength. But she was not foolhardy in approaching this decision. Once she had made her mind up, 'my back was up against the wall, I knew I could not afford the luxury of writer's block'.

Any idea of working while she wrote went out of the window when she discovered that although she was eligible to receive financial aid, she was not eligible for childcare subsidy. Joanne was therefore forced into unemployment. The author would later recall that at that point she found herself in 'an appalling poverty trap' from which it seemed almost impossible to escape.

The whole process of applying for social support was humiliating and demoralising. Once again, she was getting those disapproving looks from strangers who saw her as something to be despised.

'That was probably the lowest point in my life,' she confessed to the *Boston Globe*. 'My self-respect was on the floor. I didn't want Jessica to grow up this way, so she became my inspiration and writing about Harry became my safe haven.'

Joanne soon discovered that many of her so-called friends were suddenly not there for her. They gave her strange looks and what conversations they had with her were strained and forced. But the young woman was also grateful for her sister and the handful of friends who stuck with her when the general attitude was that Joanne was nothing more than a freeloader. If she needed a few pounds to tide her over, they were there. But more important, on those days when the writing was not going well, Jessica was a handful, and she was feeling miserable, Joanne had people around who would just sit and listen as she poured her heart out.

Welfare support barely covered rent and food, so Joanne was forced to go to great lengths to save money. There were nights when there was barely enough food for mother and child, so Joanne would go to bed hungry. She could not even afford a used typewriter and, of course, even the most outdated computer was out of the question. So she would gather up scraps of paper and any pencils she could find and write out the adventures of Harry Potter in longhand.

Another problem was where to write. Her housing benefit only covered the rent on a cold, depressing one-room flat. This was hardly the place to inspire fantasy, and it was certainly not where Joanne wanted Jessica to spend the early part of her life. The struggling writer and mother put on her thinking cap and soon formulated an ingenious way to write and make her baby happy at the same time.

Every day she would put Jessica in her baby carrier and walk her around town until the child fell asleep. She would then head for one of a number of local cafés, where for the price of a cup of espresso and a glass of water, she could sit and write for a couple of hours while her daughter slept. Years later, Joanne would marvel at how much she had managed to write in those short periods of time.

One of her regular stops was the Nicolson Café, whose co-owner, Dougal McBride, remembered how he would glance up from his work and, sure enough, there would be Joanne writing away at a corner table.

'She was quite an odd sight,' he remembered in *People*. 'She would just push the pram with one hand and write away.'

Occasionally, Joanne would be too tired or the weather would be too bleak for her to risk taking Jessica out and about, so she would be forced to write in the flat. These were the times when Joanne would think that things could not get any worse.

However, through all the tough times, Joanne was buoyed up by the good cheer she was finding in writing her novel. As the pages continued to pile up, *Harry Potter* became her imaginary white knight, righting all the wrongs in her fantasy world that could not be fixed in her own. Her eyes would grow intense and her mouth would become fixed when she was devising the latest diabolical deed for Voldemort.

And then there was wise old Dumbledore, whose every appearance in her manuscript was a time for inner joy and celebration.

'I wasn't really aware that it was a children's book,' she recalled in *Newsweek* of her feelings while writing *Harry Potter and the Philosopher's Stone*. 'I really wrote it for me. It was what I found funny and what I liked.'

As she had hoped, writing the *Harry Potter* fable was mentally and emotionally seeing her through the tough times. But as she neared the completion of the book, some of her old insecurities came flooding back. To fulfil her dream of becoming a writer, Joanne would have to risk all by sending the book out to publishers, who could dash her hopes without batting an eye.

Once she had decided that this was a risk worth taking, Joanne's next step was to decide just how one went about getting published. She had heard stories about how one needed an agent in order to be accepted by a book publisher. Now all she needed to do was find an agent.

Her first stop was the local library, where she found a writer's directory that listed the names and addresses of agents. Joanne pored over the directory and compiled a list of the agents she felt might be the most receptive to her book.

Harry Potter and the Philosopher's Stone was completed early in 1994. Joanne went over the manuscript carefully, rewriting and polishing until she finally had the book exactly as she had hoped. Because the cost of photocopying what had turned out to be an 80,000-word text was so prohibitive, Joanne, with the aid of a cheap typewriter she had managed to purchase, typed up two copies of her novel.

Then she sent the two copies to the top two agents on her list and hoped for the best.

1994 marked a turning point in Joanne's life. She had applied for and had received a grant from the Scottish Arts Council. The money was enough to allow Joanne to get proper childcare for Jessica during the day. Encouraged by this, she began looking for work and soon found a job in Edinburgh as a teacher of French at the Leith Academy and, later, at the Moray House Training College. True to her word, a year to the day that Joanne pulled into Edinburgh, penniless, she was now self-sufficient and off welfare benefits.

Joanne Rowling was feeling reborn.

In her spare time, Joanne continued to play around with *Harry Potter* and had soon come up with a storyline for a second book. She was hoping against hope that a second book would be possible. But thus far, there was nothing to convince her that it would ever come to pass.

'I had no idea truthfully what kind of reception it would get,' she explained in *School Library Journal*, 'if indeed it would ever get published, because I had never looked to publish before. I knew how difficult it would be and I was a completely unknown writer.'

One day, a letter arrived in the mail. Joanne could tell immediately it was from one of the agents to whom she had sent a copy of Harry. She was thrilled to get a response. But even as she tore open the envelope, 'I assumed it was a rejection note,' she recalled in the *Daily Telegraph*. 'But inside the envelope there was a letter saying "Thank you. We would be pleased to represent your manuscript on an exclusive basis." It was the best letter of my life. I read it eight times.'

Christopher Little was an all-business, no-frills type of person. But this unsolicited manuscript by a totally unknown writer had touched him. It was very well written, the story was entertaining and, like Joanne, he sensed that *Harry Potter and the Philosopher's Stone* was not entirely a children's book.

On meeting her, Christopher Little was also impressed with her enthusiasm and her struggle against formidable odds to get the book written. He also liked her grasp of reality. From his experience, Little knew that most children's authors struggle to make £2,000 a year and that they rarely end up becoming well known.

'When I went into this, my agent said to me, "I don't want you going away from this meeting thinking you're going to make a fortune,"' Joanne reported to *School Library Journal*. 'Then I said to him, "I know I'm not going to make any money out of it. I know I'm not going to be famous." All I ever wanted was for somebody to publish Harry so I could go to bookshops and see it.'

Christopher Little began sending out *Harry Potter and the Philosopher's Stone* to some of the biggest publishers in England. And as he had predicted, it was a long, hard road to publication. Before long, the first of a seemingly endless stream of rejections arrived at the agent's door. Some of the reasons given for not wanting to publish the book were that it was too long, too slow or too literary. Joanne was disappointed but was encouraged by Little's assessment that the book was too good not to be picked up at some point.

Joanne went about her business of being a mother and a teacher and tried to put the unenthusiastic reception to Harry out of her thoughts. But during the next year, she would often find herself day-dreaming about spying her book in the front window of the local bookshop. During those moments, she would find herself smiling at the events in her life that had brought her to this point.

In 1996, *Harry Potter and the Philosopher's Stone* finally found a home with British publisher Bloomsbury. Joanne was beside herself with joy when she heard the news. 'It was comparable only to having my daughter.'

True to Christopher Little's prediction, Bloomsbury offered the modest amount of £2,000.

'That was totally OK with me,' Joanne stated. 'All I wanted was to be able to support myself writing so I wouldn't have to give it up.'

As often happens in the publishing industry, word of mouth about the merit of the new book was good. Within months of Bloomsbury's purchase, inquiries from publishers all over the world began pouring in.

In 1997, the overwhelming interest in this children's book by an unknown writer had reached such a level that an auction was arranged at the time of the annual Bologna Book Fair held in Italy, at which foreign rights to books are sold. Joanne had been so thrilled at the prospect of Harry being published in her native England that she had paid only scant attention to what had been going on elsewhere in the world.

But she laughed when she recalled in *Salon* magazine the night her telephone rang at around 8.00pm. It was Christopher Little calling long-distance from New York.

'He said there was an auction taking place. An auction? I thought, Sotheby's, Christie's ...? Antiques? What is this all about? Then I realised that it was my book that was being auctioned off.'

At that very moment, thousands of miles away in a crowded room at the Bologna Book Fair, editorial director Arthur A Levine was about to take the biggest gamble of his life. The bidding on *Harry Potter and the Philosopher's Stone* had been in tense and the amounts being put up for the US rights had already reached astronomical levels. Levine, a spirited man with a ready smile, was about to make a bid that could change his life for ever.

'It's a scary thing when you keep

bidding and the stakes are getting higher and higher,' said Levine in the *New York Times*. 'It's one thing to say I love this first novel by this unknown woman in Scotland and I want to publish it. It's another thing as the bidding goes higher. Do you love it this much? Do you love it at $50,000? At $70,000?'

The reason for Levine's concern was that the bidding was back to him and he was faced with the decision of offering an unheard-of bid of $100,000.

'I had never paid so much for an acquisition before. It was a great risk. If people believe in you and you flop, then you walk out on the plank and plunge.'

Little called Joanne again at 10.00pm that same evening. 'He said I should get ready because a Mr Levine of the *Scholastic Press* would pay a six-figure sum for the book and would be ringing me in a little bit. I nearly died.'

The tension mounted in Joanne's

tiny Edinburgh flat. She was excited and scared all at the same time. She had hoped, under ideal circumstances, that a modest US sale would allow her to continue to write and teach on a part-time basis. But, she reasoned, things seemed to be moving much faster than anybody had expected.

The telephone rang promptly at 11.00pm. At the other end of the line, Levine was determined not to put any undue pressure on his new author. But his voice was shaking with excitement as he said hello.

'I called her very late,' he told the *New York Times*, 'and we had a very nice conversation. I said, "Don't be scared," and she said, "Thanks, I am." And we both said now that we've paid this much, we had to concentrate on making the book work.'

It was well past midnight when Joanne, after checking on her sleeping daughter, finally went to bed.

'But I couldn't sleep. On one level, I

was obviously delighted,' she told a *Salon* magazine reporter. 'But most of me was just frozen in terror.'

7

HARRY CONQUERS THE WORLD

*J*oanne had good reason to be fearful in the weeks following her big signing with Scholastic Books.

The amount of money involved was so unheard of in children's book circles that the book publishing gossip was that Arthur Levine and Scholastic had taken leave of their senses. Many pessimists predicted that no matter how good the book was, it would certainly not make anywhere near enough to earn back the massive advance.

Joanne's agent and Arthur Levine assured her that Scholastic Books was not in the habit of laying out huge amounts of money for books they felt would fail. Joanne was not completely convinced. But that was only part of her concern.

Word of this author who had landed an unprecedented advance for a children's book had quickly spread around the world. The normally shy woman was now being deluged with requests for interviews and her picture was appearing in newspapers and magazines. And this was before her book was even published in Great Britain.

If it had been up to her, Joanne would have done no publicity for the book at all. But she felt a strong sense of loyalty to those who had taken this chance with her, so she agreed to every request.

'The stakes had seemed to have gone up a lot,' she told an interviewer in 1999. 'I attracted a lot of publicity for which I was totally unprepared.'

Joanne was not big on change, and the idea of doing interviews in stuffy hotel rooms and television studios ran contrary to her nature. So when she started entertaining the press, she would gently insist that, whenever possible, interviews be done at her familiar table in the Nicholson Café.

When these interviews took place, a crowd of waiters and waitresses would stand on the periphery listening. They would smile as Joanne explained how she would sit at this very table and write under the most trying of conditions. Many of them had served her when she was down on her luck. Now they were as proud as they could possibly be that their regular customer was a well-known author.

Initially, she was not comfortable doing interviews. Joanne was not always fluent in her responses and worried about the kind of impression she was making. But she knew only how to be honest, and the press were going to make of that what they would.

Much of that early publicity put Joanne on the defensive. In many newspaper and magazine interviews, the reporters painted a picture of Joanne as a penniless, divorced single mother living on welfare and writing at her leisure in cafés. She had no problem with the accuracy and, yes, it was true. But she felt 'knocked sideways' by the negative image it presented of her and the fact that it was forcing her to relive what she considered one of the saddest periods of her life.

Joanne was quick to clarify that she had been gainfully employed since 1990, when she started writing Harry, and that the only reason she had to go on welfare was that the system in Edinburgh would not allow for childcare. And then, she insisted, it was only for the year that she was completing the book.

As *Harry Potter and the Philosopher's Stone* was going through the publishing process in England, Joanne found that there was one more compromise she was being asked to make. The publishers, fearful that a book with a woman's name on the cover might not attract young boys, asked if Joanne would mind if she were listed as JK Rowling. Joanne thought it was an odd request but saw no harm in going along with the notion.

Harry Potter and the Philosopher's Stone was published in England in 1997. The book was an immediate smash hit, selling more than 150,000 copies in a matter of months. Reviewers fell over themselves in praise of the book.

One critic stated, 'The book is an unassailable stand for the power of fresh, innovative storytelling.' Another commented, 'Rowling's ability to put a fantastic spin on sports, student rivalry and eccentric faculty contributes to the humour, charm and delight of her utterly captivating story.'

By the end of the year, JK Rowling's first novel had garnered up a number of prestigious awards, including the Nestlé Smarties Book Prize, the Federation of Children's Books Group Award and the British Book Awards Children's Book of the Year. A little into 1998, the book had sold a total of half a million copies, an unprecedented number for a children's book.

Joanne was thrilled and more than a bit amused at what was happening with Harry. She was hard-pressed to answer the question she often asked as a child. Why?

'I suppose it's mainly word of mouth,' she suggested in response to the book's success in the *Guardian*. 'I think children just tell one another about it.'

But she did have a good laugh at the notion that the reason so many books were being sold was because a good many of them were being snapped up by adults just as eager to read the adventures of Harry as their children. As an example, she cited a story she had heard from a friend who had seen a man in a suit on a train reading a copy behind his newspaper.

'I had not aimed the books at children,' she once said. 'I only wrote them for me.'

With the money from her US book deal and another eight countries rolling in, Joanne was slowly beginning to adjust to the idea of not being poor. But it did not come in one handy lump sum. She agonised for a long time whether to purchase a £75 coat so that she would look smart for her television appearances.

But with the success of *Harry Potter and the Philosopher's Stone* in England and the American edition due out shortly, Joanne decided it was time to leave poverty behind her. The first thing she did was rent a house in Edinburgh. Nothing fancy, just well-lit rooms, heating and comfortable furniture. However, for Joanne, it was pure heaven and relief.

'I no longer have the constant worry of whether Jessica will outgrow a pair of shoes before I've got the money for the next pair,' she said in a *Daily Telegraph* article.

Joanne was already hard at work on the follow-up to *Harry Potter and the Philosopher's Stone* before it had been published. So when she was not handling the increasing demand for interviews or tending to her daughter, Joanne was churning out pages of what would ultimately be titled *Harry Potter and the Chamber of Secrets*. But while she was now able to afford a computer and Jessica was of an age where she was spending part of the day in pre-school, little of Joanne's approach to writing had changed.

Every day, after kissing her daughter goodbye, Joanne would walk down to Nicholson's Café, pull up a chair at a table next to an upstairs window, pull out paper and a pen, and begin writing. The first time she did this after her first book had been accepted, the waiter, who had served her regularly when she was down and out, did a double take when she asked for a menu. One reason for continuing the routine was that Joanne felt lonely at the prospect of sitting in her house, by herself, in front of a computer.

'Writing and cafés are strongly linked in my brain,' she recently revealed to the press. 'I still write in longhand. I like physically shuffling around with papers.'

Harry Potter and the Chamber of Secrets was almost complete and ready for publication when the US edition of *Harry Potter and the Philosopher's Stone* was available in August 1998. The British mania for *Harry Potter* was soon duplicated in the USA as children and adults fell in love with Harry and his adventures.

Soon, editions of Joanne's first book were published in nearly 30 other countries. Joanne would have a giggle at the different languages and, in some cases, the different cover designs which bound the books. As each new edition was released, her happiness increased.

Publishers on both sides of the Atlantic were now convinced that *Harry Potter* was no fluke, so contracts were quickly drawn up that would have Joanne writing a total of seven *Harry Potter* books in the coming years. Joanne was thrilled. Then she was scared to death.

In a practical sense, the longevity of the contract meant she would never want for anything for her daughter or herself. But there were also what she described as 'a few weeks of terror' as she contemplated whether she could write the remainder of the books with the same enthusiasm now that the whole world was looking over her shoulder.

To relieve the fear of writer's block, Joanne sat down and plotted out the remaining five *Harry Potter* books. She was painstaking in figuring out the storylines, the specific elements of each adventure, and the important message that readers young and old would take away from each book. At the end of this plotting session, Joanne emerged confident in her ability to finish Harry Potter's education.

'And I finally realised what the most important thing for me was,' she stated in the *Boston Globe*. 'I love writing these books. I don't think anyone could enjoy reading them more than I enjoy writing them.'

Harry Potter and the Chamber of Secrets was published in July 1998 and, like its predecessor, was an immediate blockbuster all over the world. In the UK alone, the book outsold the latest novels by bestselling writers such as John Grisham and Tom Clancy.

Joanne continued to be amazed at the way people had taken Harry Potter and his world to their hearts and minds. But the writer was also finding that those bestselling books were also beginning to complicate her life. Already well into writing her third book, *Harry Potter and the Prisoner of Azkaban*, Joanne was finding that she had less time to write because of interviews, book signings and various lectures and school appearances.

Joanne was a good sport when it came to things like that. In the case of the book signings and appearances at schools, she loved the idea of actually meeting with the children who were reading her books.

'As an ex-teacher, it's just so liberating to go in front of a class simply to entertain them and it's great when they've read the books and can quote you passages and know the characters,' she said in the *Guardian*.

But there were also those days when things did not go according to plan and Joanne found herself overwhelmed to the point of tears. During what seemed like an endless round of promotional duties surrounding the release of *Harry Potter and the Chamber of Secrets*, Joanne was having trouble checking out of a London hotel. At first, the hotel would not allow her to check out because there was no record of her name in the computer. Finally, a hotel manager found her name but insisted that she could not leave until she had paid her bill. This upset the normally unflappable Joanne because she knew that her publisher had already sorted it out. With the hotel confusion finally straightened out, she hopped into a taxi, now quite late for an interview. Half-way there, Joanne realised that she had left the hotel without her purse.

It was all too much. Joanne burst into tears, startling the taxi driver.

However, generally, her good humour and sunny outlook carried Joanne through the difficulty of being in the public eye. She felt incredibly fortunate to be in this position because it had come as a result of her unwillingness to give up on her dream. So, yes, she would give interviews and talk to people about Harry until the cows came home.

But at the end of the day, she would happily race home to comfort Jessica. As she held her young daughter and asked about her day at school, Joanne was proud — proud that as her mother, she was able to provide Jessica with security and a good life.

And if there was time, Joanne would walk down to Nicholson's Café, where she might find a few moments to write. She would sometimes order the usual espresso and water. But, just as often, she would also pick up the menu, and without worrying about the price, choose something to eat.

8

HARRY EVER AFTER

Harry Potter and the Prisoner of Azkaban was published late in 1998. The mania for Harry continued as the book immediately followed its predecessors to the top of the world's bestseller lists.

Reporters once again came around, hoping the quiet author of these fantastic adventures would be able to supply the background to Harry Potter's continued success. And, once again, Joanne found it hard to come up with an answer that did not have the words 'shocked and amazed' somewhere in it.

Happily, Joanne was more than willing to try.

'I am still stunned that I went from being an unknown writer on the bread-line to having my books at the top of the charts. It's truly amazing,' she would regularly tell reporters.

But not all the news was good. A number of religious groups had decided that the *Harry Potter* books were endorsing evil themes and attitudes. Many of these groups sent letters to newspapers objecting to the books and, in some cases, they tried to have the books banned from libraries and bookstores.

Joanne was upset by their actions but chose to ignore them. Eventually, the storm of protest passed.

Joanne celebrated New Year's Eve 1999 quietly with a small group of friends.

At the stroke of midnight, she toasted her good fortune and her good friends. She could only imagine what the forthcoming year would offer.

A resolution was not long in coming. Nobody had ever referred to Joanne as a workaholic. But as fast as the new Harry books were coming out, one had to wonder if Joanne did anything but write. She repeatedly stated that writing was the thing she most liked to do. However, she did decide that she owed it to herself and Jessica to get away every once in a while. So she began travelling, taking short jaunts to neighbouring countries that would allow Jessica and her to explore pastures new and escape the distractions that were always a phone call away in Edinburgh.

It came as no surprise that Hollywood was soon wild about Harry as well. Movie-makers immediately saw the possibilities of *Harry Potter* as a movie. No fewer than a dozen film studios were actively pursuing the rights to turn *Harry Potter* into a full-length motion picture. Once again, Joanne was glued to the telephone as Christopher Little relayed the latest messages regarding a film contract. But the negotiation of film deals, unlike that of book deals, tend to drag on for ages, so Joanne was content to continue with the business of writing the fourth instalment of *Harry Potter*.

With two books out in the same year, Joanne was given more time to devise Harry's latest adventure. There had been some concern from the publisher that writing two books literally back to back might have put a bit of a strain on their favourite author. However, Joanne was nothing if not anxious, after the seemingly endless round of press and publicity, to get back to creating another exciting *Harry Potter* adventure for her legion of fans.

The routine remained pretty much the same. Although her notoriety had made the Nicholson Café a sudden tourist attraction, and Joanne would occasionally find herself feeling self-conscious at being gawped at by people who had come to watch her work, she would still find time to sit and work there a few hours almost every day. But, out of necessity, she was also working in other cafés and pubs, which she wisely refused to name.

Wherever she went, the writing continued to go smoothly. The characters had become like a second family to her. She knew what would work and what would appear false. Creating new names for her outlandish characters was always a joy. But Joanne had to admit that with this book, things were beginning to change. Harry and the other characters were now well into their teenage years. She felt it was time to have Harry discover girls.

This was an exciting turn of events

for Joanne, one that allowed her to revisit her own adolescence as a blueprint for how Harry should react the first time he sees a girl as something other than a good buddy. Harry was never boring, but now there was an extra element of excitement that would have Joanne snatching up her pen and paper at every opportunity.

Shortly before the turn of the New Year 2000, Joanne, with Jessica by her side, boarded a plane at London's Heathrow Airport and headed for the USA on a three-week book tour. These were exciting times for Joanne. She had heard about how well the first three books had done in America, but she was anxious to meet with her readers face to face and experience the joy and excitement they had for her work with her own eyes.

At each and every stop on this cross-country tour, Joanne was very much the teacher in her dealings with the thousands of fans who lined up to see her. She would encourage them to read and write as often as possible. She would chuckle at the inevitable question on how to pronounce her name before saying, 'It's Roe-ling, not Row-ling.' The woman of simple tastes grew to like the rock-star treatment she was receiving with limo rides and high security at every stop. The look on Joanne's face was worth a thousand words. But only one was really necessary — joy.

The year 2000 would bring continued success for Joanne. *Harry Potter and the Goblet of Fire* was ready for an 8 July publication date. It was also announced during this period that Warner Brothers had secured the rights to make the movie version of *Harry Potter and the Philosopher's Stone*. Originally, the studio had stated that Steven Spielberg was interested in directing the film. But the director would later bow out of the project, saying, 'My directorial interests were taking me in another direction.' Eventually, the studio made its choice and assigned a talented director, Chris Columbus, and a screenwriter, Steven Kloves, to adapt Joanne's fantasy world to the screen.

Joanne agreed to Warner Brothers' offer on the condition that she would have input into the screenplay and that the movie would be live action rather than animation. But as the studio officially announced that *Harry Potter* would be in cinemas by in the summer of 2001, she had to admit to being nervous about the prospect of seeing Harry on the big screen.

'It's actually a mixture of excitement and nervousness,' she said upon hearing the good news. 'I do think Harry would make a great film. But obviously I do feel protective toward the characters I've lived for with so long.'

In March, director Columbus flew to Scotland, where he and Joanne met. Both came away from the meeting enthusiastic about the film.

'I'm terribly excited,' said Columbus in the *Los Angeles Times*. 'My oldest daughter, Eleanor, who is ten, got me into the books over a year ago. Between my four kids and their friends, I've heard a lot about what this movie should be and how I could ruin it if I cut this or that scene. I won't let anyone down. It will be a faithful adaptation.'

Joanne was also in good spirits about her sudden involvement in the movie business.

'I'm more involved than I thought I would be. I can't wait to see how they will pull off a Quidditch game.'

The publicity campaign for the release of *Harry Potter and the Goblet of Fire* reached massive proportions as the days counted down to the official publication date. At this point, Joanne was not looking forward to answering the same questions over and over again; she had in recent months started saying 'No' to all but the most important publicity events just so she would have time to write.

Her publishers took the hint and, in late spring, announced that Joanne would do one 90-minute interview session in London and that would be it. Soon, journalists from all over the world were flying in for the opportunity to ask the world's most popular author questions about her new book and her life in general.

Joanne was a bit nervous at the prospect of facing so many reporters at the same time and was concerned that this massive press conference would get out of control. But much of the questioning turned out to be highly predictable. There were the usual questions about why Harry had proven to be so popular, Joanne's struggles in Edinburgh, and how she was coping with success. Joanne fielded them with ease and responded with good humour and concisely. But there were some surprise announcements along the way.

Joanne revealed that an important character would die in the fourth book and that Harry would develop his first crush on a girl. The author also hinted that, in the fifth book, readers would finally discover why Harry continues to spend his summers with the frightful Dursleys.

The secretive author also stated that Harry's parents would not return and that she had decided long ago that magic could not bring back the dead. But she did hint that Harry's parents would continue to be an important part of future books.

Joanne left the press conference relieved that the most difficult aspect of the whole exercise was once again behind her. Now she could get back to the fun part — the writing itself.

Joanne continued to feel anxious as 8 July got closer and closer. At this point, nobody was betting against the fact that *Harry Potter and the Goblet of Fire* would do as well, if not better, than her previous three books. But Joanne was never one to take anything for granted.

Finally, the date arrived and Joanne crossed her fingers as her latest *Harry Potter* adventure went on sale in the UK and the USA at the same time. Within hours, the first reports began to come in. Bookstores were selling out of copies in a matter of minutes and were already on the telephone to re-order. Within days, the book was high up on the bestseller charts around the world. Joanne heaved a sigh of relief at the news.

The magic of *Harry Potter* was as strong as ever.

Joanne saw the summer of 2000 come and go in a state of undisguised happiness. She was already hard at work on the next *Harry* instalment. She was happy and healthy, and she had a wonderful daughter to boot.

But with the beginning of book number five, the end was now in sight. Harry Potter would graduate from his seven years of schooling at Hogwarts some time around the year 2003. And although she would occasionally tease the public about 'never say never' when asked if she would follow Harry off to college, the author has remained adamant that Harry Potter will end with book number seven.

She has admitted to feeling sad at the idea that Harry's adventures will end one day and feels that there will be a 'bereavement' when she has written the last line on the final page. But she insists that 'there will be no Harry Potter midlife crisis or Harry Potter as an old wizard'.

But as she nears the end of the year 2000, Joanne could not be happier. Her career has exceeded all her expectations.

She has a beautiful daughter and she is making a living doing what she loves to do. And she is not sad at the fact that there is no man in her life. Her feeling on that topic is that if Mr Perfect were to come along, she would be thrilled.

'But it's not my top priority,' she told *Salon* magazine. 'Right now my life is very fulfilled.'

While her future after *Harry Potter* is still up in the air, the author knows that writing will be at the centre of it. It is all she knows, and she feels putting pen to paper is necessary for her. Joanne once admitted that 'I don't feel normal when I haven't written for a while.'

Joanne has hinted many times that her next step after Harry would be to write more adult novels. But she is honest enough to accept that she will probably never write anything as popular as Harry, and that is all right with her.

'I will have lived with Harry for 13

years and I know I'll probably have to take some time off to grieve. But then I'll be on with the next book.'

What that will be is anybody's guess, including Joanne's. But she knows where she will go for inspiration. 'I might just get on another train.'

HOW ROWLING WRITES

*J*K Rowling has a simple rule when it comes to sitting down to write her latest adventure of *Harry Potter*: 'I write any time, any place, and in longhand.'

Joanne has often said that it takes her about a year to write a *Harry Potter* book. She has said that a key to turning out a full-length book in that period of time is to be consistent.

'I write nearly every day. Some days I write for ten or eleven hours. Other days I might only write for three hours. It really depends on how fast the ideas are coming to me.'

Having long ago decided that the Harry Potter books would be a seven-book series, Joanne has each storyline already well plotted before she sits down to write the book. 'I always have a basic plot line. But I like to leave some things to be decided when I write. It's more fun that way.'

Also a lot of fun are the strange-sounding names that Joanne incorporates into her tales. 'Some of the names come from folklore, and many of the names are invented.'

'I also collect unusual names and I take them from all sorts of different places. I remember that I came up with the names of the houses at Hogwarts while flying and ended up writing them on the back of an aeroplane sick bag.'

An increasingly difficult aspect of writing the *Harry Potter* books has been how to bring new readers up to speed on the previous events of the series. Joanne has said that, in *Harry Potter and the Chamber of Secrets*, it was relatively easy to fill new readers in on Harry and his first year at Hogwarts.

'But by the time I reach book five and six, this is going to be much harder,' she has said. 'Maybe what I'll do is just write a preface that says 'Previously in *Harry Potter* ...' and tell readers to go back and read books one through four.'

Joanne is often asked by youngsters how they can begin to write. Her first suggestion has always been to read everything and anything to get an idea of how writers write. But when it is time to pick up the pencil, the writer has suggested in many interviews that kids use their own lives as a starting point.

'Start by writing the things that you know. Write about your own experiences and your own feelings. That's what I do.'

About the Author

Marc Shapiro has been a freelance entertainment journalist for more than 25 years, covering film, television and music for a number of national and international newspapers and magazines. He is the author of more than a dozen celebrity biographies, including *Freddie Prinze Jr: The Unofficial Biography*; *Love Story: The Unauthorized Biography of Jennifer Love Hewitt*; and *Lucy Lawless: Warrior Princess*. He lives in Pasadena, California, with his wife Nancy, daughter Rachael, dog Keri, and cats Bad Baby and Chaos.